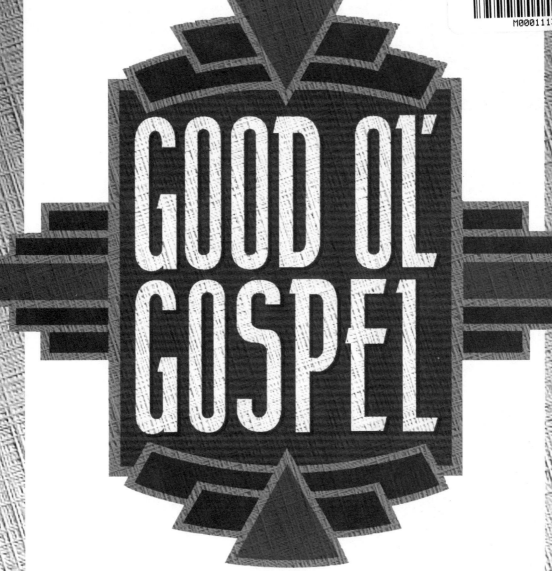

GOOD OL' GOSPEL

35 ALL-TIME FAVORITE SONGS

BY MOSIE LISTER

WITH HISTORICAL FACTS, PHOTOS, AND SONG STORIES

Lillenas PUBLISHING COMPANY

KANSAS CITY, MO 64141

CONTENTS

Mosie Lister
Over 50 Years in Gospel Music

Growing Up

When people meet Mosie Lister, they can't help but wonder where all his great songs came from. How were they born, and how did he get started writing in the first place? Here are his own words:

"I've always loved gospel music. I don't remember a time when my mind was not full of music. As early as five years old, I wanted very badly to write music. My family enjoyed singing—my father taught music, and my mother played the piano—so our home was always full of music. We sang when we had nothing to do, we sang for church, we sang for everything we could sing for. We used to sit around the house and just sing a cappella and listen to each other. Those growing up days when the house was so full of music were just wonderful to me."

Mosie was born on September 8, 1921, in Cochran, Georgia, the second son of Willis W. Lister and Pearl Holland Lister. He learned to read music almost as soon as he learned to read. His early performing experiences came as part of a family group that included his parents, his older brother Walter Olan, and his younger sister Margery.

When Mosie was age 9, the Lister family moved to a farm, where they lived until he was 19. Farm life fed his creative inclinations:

"In the days when I was helping my father in the work on the family farm, there was much time during the day to let my imagination roam. And being so caught up in gospel music, I naturally gave a lot of thought to composition.

"I loved to mentally hear huge choirs singing new songs, accompanied by orchestras of similar size. By the age of 16-17 years, I could now and then imagine a complete song.

"More than once my father left what he was doing and looked for me, to see what I might be doing, and found me beneath a tree writing a song, with the mule tied nearby. I think he was indignant, and I guess perhaps I was not using the time very well. But it made sense to me and was just a natural thing to do. I had heard the song in my imagination and just wanted to get it written down."

Music Studies

When he was nine, Mosie began learning music theory from his father, who taught music as a hobby. But music didn't always come easy. In the early years he had trouble distinguishing pitches, and his parents felt he was tone deaf.

When he was 12, they started him on violin lessons with Miss Tiny Gibbs. She was a wonderful, patient teacher, and her lessons greatly helped Mosie's sense of pitch. Early in the lessons she even transcribed certain pieces for him to practice. More than anything else, she instilled in him a genuine love for the classics. As a result, he loved the violin, playing it for hours in the evening when his chores were done.

Mosie on the front porch of his grandfather John Lister's home in 1936. "One of my favorite places playing one of my favorite instruments."

In school, Mosie was an excellent student. But ironically, he was weakest in writing. Putting his thoughts down on paper, even doing a book report, was a real struggle. Writing was one of the last professions his teachers would have chosen for him.

Jesus Is Coming Soon

Mosie Lister

Grady Thomas

Mosie Lister's first published song, which appeared in the collection *Joy Divine*, published by James D. Vaughan, Music Publisher, in 1941. Grady Thomas, who taught Mosie composition briefly during a trip through middle Georgia, took his student's song and rewrote the music, keeping Mosie's lyrics.

But music was in his blood. Fresh out of high school, at age 16, Mosie tried hard to get into country music. He had transferred his violin lessons into country fiddle and guitar. Soon he was one of the top-ranked fiddle players in Georgia, winning virtually every contest he entered. Mosie remembers, "I liked the crowds, the applause. I thought, 'This is it.'"

But the next year, Mosie became a Christian, and his desire for a career in country music began to fade. "I realized that God had a plan for my life and that that plan involved my being able to create gospel music. All I ever really wanted to do was just communicate the gospel to the world. That was my most heartfelt prayer when I was 17. I spent a year asking God to help me learn to do that. At that time, I didn't really care if I wrote gospel music or if I wrote music of some other form. I just wanted to communicate the gospel."

To further that desire, in January 1939, Mosie traveled to the Vaughan School of Music in Lawrenceburg, Tennessee. There he studied harmony with the likes of Adger M. Pace, the composer of gospel songs like "Jesus Is All I Need," and G. T. Speer, father of Ben and Brock Speer.

His Early Quartet Days

Mosie's first involvement in a gospel quartet came in 1941, while still living with his parents. He was invited to sing with the Sunny South Quartet. Gladly accepting, he moved to Tampa, Florida, to join Clyde Cain, Horace Floyd, Lee Kitchens, and pianist R. D. Ginnett.

The Sunny South Quartet in 1941. L. to R.: Mosie Lister, Clyde Cain, Horace Floyd, Lee Kitchens, and R. D. Ginnett.

But World War II put the group on hold, and Mosie entered the U.S. Navy. He served on a subchaser in the Gulf of Mexico and in the Caribbean, then went to North Africa in 1943 where he stayed until after the Italian invasion.

He recalls many times when he could have been placed in life-threatening situations, but the Lord's hand seemed to be on him. For his last year in the service, he was transferred to the Officer Training School in Troy, New York, where he studied engineering at the Rensselaer Polytechnic Institute.

Mosie Lister in the U.S. Navy, 1942

After his discharge, Mosie attended Middle Georgia College for about a year, then returned to the Sunny South Quartet. By now, the personnel were slightly different. Quentin Hicks replaced R. D. Ginnett on the piano, and instead of Clyde Cain, Jim "Chief" Wetherington sang bass.

The 1946 version of the Sunny South Quartet. L. to R.: Horace Floyd, tenor; Lee Kitchens, lead; Mosie Lister, baritone; Jim "Chief" Wetherington, bass; Quentin Hicks, piano.

"Chief" became a force in shaping Mosie's song-writing: "He and I came to know each other quite well. As a matter of fact, his personality and his voice tremendously influenced a lot of my songs. I understood not only what he was able to do physically but what he liked to do."

Mosie also became close friends with another member of the Sunny South Quartet, Lee Kitchens. In June 1946, they shared a double wedding, with Mosie marrying Miss Wylene Whitten of Tampa, Florida. Mosie and Wylene were blessed with twin daughters, Brenda Sue and Barbara Lynn, in November 1949.

The Melody Masters

Lee, Mosie, and "Chief" soon established a group of their own, the Melody Masters. Alvin Tootle joined them to sing first tenor, with Wally Varner at the piano. Mosie recalls, "It turned out to be an almost magical combination. They wanted to be experimental and innovative. I enjoyed writing so much that I started inventing new ideas and new sounds, and some new ways to change keys. I started searching for fresh material for them and writing some songs for them that were different from what other quartets were doing. As a matter of fact, some of the ideas that we developed became part of the ingredients that later were so important to the Statesmen Quartet."

The Melody Masters, Tampa, Florida, 1947. Wally Varner at the piano; standing, L. to R.: Alvin Tootle, first tenor; Lee Kitchens, lead; Mosie Lister, baritone; Jim "Chief" Wetherington, bass.

The Statesmen Quartet

Mosie Lister first met Hovie Lister in 1946 when the latter was playing piano for the Rangers Quartet. (Though the two share both a last name and lots of years in gospel music, they are no relation.) Mosie remembers, "He and I instantly liked each other. He said he would like to start a quartet of his own someday and asked me if I'd like to be a part of it. I told him that I certainly would."

Hovie also took to Mosie from the beginning. "My impression of Mosie Lister the first time I met him was that he was a very smart, astute, and yet very reserved musician. Mosie was not excitable or not the kind of guy that would just chime in with 'Hey, listen to this song!' He thought through all the songs he wrote. He thought through the theology of the songs, the harmony—he was very careful about everything he did. I think that stemmed from a lot of things: from his personal relationship with the Lord; his extreme knowledge of music; and the fact that Mosie was a perfectionist."

Mosie had developed vocal problems, the result of a serious respiratory problem. The doctors advised him to totally quit singing for a year—advice that Mosie had alternately taken and ignored. But fearing that he would have to give up singing and find a new occupation, Mosie moved to Atlanta on the promise of a job with Rich's Department Store.

Hovie was also living in Atlanta and had become friends with the son of the owner of the *Atlanta Constitution*. They had just built a new radio station. Through that connection, Hovie got a radio program and began conversations with Mosie in earnest about assembling a quartet. Together they formed the original Statesmen. Mosie remembers: "What a wonderful sound! We had Hovie's hyperactive mind and his stage pres-

The original Statesmen Quartet, 1948. Standing: Bervin Kendrick, lead; Hovie Lister, piano; Mosie Lister, baritone. Seated: A. D. Soward, bass; Bobby Strickland, first tenor.

ence. They were just a bunch of good guys who enjoyed singing the gospel."

But Mosie soon decided that traveling was not the life for him. He stepped out of his singing duties with the Statesmen but stayed on as their songwriter and arranger. Jake Hess was hired from the Melody Masters as his replacement, and "Chief" Wetherington came over as well. Like "Chief," Jake's voice and personality became a major influence in Mosie's writing. They were later joined by Denver Crumpler and Doy Ott. Mosie remembers that particular group of Statesmen:

"They were the best version of the Statesmen ever, in my mind. They enjoyed practicing and were always willing to try something a little different. They worked hard to perfect certain sounds, even little nuances that might improve what they were doing and set them apart. During those years they practiced almost every day, and I was able to spend a couple of hours with them every morning."

The Statesmen had a 6 A.M. broadcast on WCON Radio in Atlanta. After the broadcast, Mosie would join them. They would walk up to the S & W Cafeteria, eat breakfast together, then come back and rehearse. Often Mosie would bring a new song or a new arrangement of an old song. They would go through the piece, and Mosie would gradually refine it until it worked just right. At noon they had another live radio broadcast, after which they would drive to that evening's concert.

"Sometimes we sort of invented sounds on the spot. So many of the songs I wrote back in those days were closely involved with their overall sound. I deliberately tried to shape the songs I was writing around what they were able to do and what they enjoyed doing. If they wanted to sing something that sounded contemporary and advanced for that time, and they did, I would just go home and develop something in my study and give it back to them."

Among the numerous songs written especially for the Statesmen were "Goodby, World, Goodby," "Happy Rhythm," "I'll Leave It All Behind," "I'm Bound for the Kingdom," "Nothing Can Compare," "If You Believe," and "Sunday Meetin' Time." Mosie was writing a lot during those days, and the Statesmen were singing almost everything he wrote.

Not only was the group a major influence on Mosie's writing, but the reverse was also true. Hovie says of Mosie, "I give him credit as having molded the early years of the Statesmen Quartet's existence."

In 1953, the Statesmen were traveling home from a concert when their Packard limousine collided with another auto. It tumbled end over end twice, then four more times sideways. The only casualty was Doy Ott's nose, which needed surgical repair. While he was out, Mosie filled in for him, since he was writing most of their arrangements and knew all the parts well. This photo was taken during that time: L. to R.: Cat Freeman, tenor; Jake Hess, lead; Mosie Lister, baritone; Jim "Chief" Wetherington, bass; Hovie Lister, piano.

In those early years, the quartets were not big business. It was a tough, very demanding life. But the members struggled through it together, and lasting relationships were formed. Mosie became friends for life with men like Hovie Lister, Jake Hess, J. D. Sumner, Wally Varner, and "Chief" Wetherington.

Elvis Presley

The Statesmen, however, did become rather popular. Soon they were traveling with the Blackwood Brothers, singing somewhere nearly every night. During those years, Hovie remembers meeting Elvis Presley as an unknown youth about 14 years of age. Elvis was a big fan of the Statesmen, and whenever they were close enough, he would come to their concerts and hang around backstage.

It was there that he learned the gospel songs that he would later record. Hovie says that Elvis knew enough Mosie Lister songs to fill an entire album. He eventually recorded three: "His Hand in Mine," "He Knows Just What I Need," and "Where No One Stands Alone." "His Hand in Mine" became the title song of Elvis' first gospel album. Elvis won a Grammy for that album, the only Grammy he would ever win.

Hovie remembers one night in particular:

"Elvis had already been in the army and had come back. He had made several movies and was real, real popular. About once every month the Statesmen and the Blackwood Brothers would sing in Memphis. If Elvis was in town, he would come down and enter through the backdoor, along with his entourage of bodyguards, and would sit backstage.

"One night he came in, and we were onstage. I was sitting with the piano facing backstage, with the audience on my right. Well, I was facing Elvis, so he came in and said, 'Where No One Stands Alone.' We had about five minutes left in our time, and I was trying to wrap up our program. Naturally I was getting ready for my finale, so I was getting ready for a fast song—something that would stir the crowd. And every time he would say, 'Where No One Stands Alone' and 'How Long Has It Been?' I could read his lips, but I would just shake him off—like a pitcher does a catcher—and go ahead with my program. We did 'Get Away, Jordan,' which was a sugarstick, a fast song, one of those animated things where I jumped off the stage and everything.

"When I got through, everybody up on stage was taking a bow and we were just tearing that place up. We were bent over bowing, and we couldn't see what was going on, just hearing the crowd applaud. I thought, 'My word, we made a hit tonight!' All of a sudden I felt a hand on my shoulder. I turned around, and it was Elvis, and no one had known he was there. He turned to me and said, 'Tell Jake to leave the stage. We are going to do "How Long Has It Been?" and "Where No One Stands Alone."' So he sang those two songs, and it absolutely tore up the audience. It was tremendous. They were on their feet the whole time he sang both songs."

Elvis was not the only major artist to record Mosie's songs. For example, "Where No One Stands Alone" has been recorded by over 60 artists, including many of the biggest names in country and Christian music. Among them were Loretta Lynn, the Blackwood Brothers, Porter Wagoner, the Chuck Wagon Gang, Don Gibson, Ferlin Husky, the Oak Ridge Boys, George Beverly Shea, Merle Haggard, Jimmie Davis, and Floyd Cramer. In 1990, the song was inducted into SESAC's Hall of Fame.

Mosie Lister Publications

Mosie had had a deep compulsion to write songs, even from earliest childhood. And ever since he had committed his life to the Lord at age 17, he had prayed that God would use him.

But the path to full-time ministry was neither quick nor smooth. Mosie explains: "At times I would get away from what God wanted me to do with my life. But each time, God would pick me up and put me back where I ought to be."

He held numerous jobs over the years. In Tampa in the mid-1940s, he owned a record store for about a year. It was a relief to him when the business finally failed. Later, while singing for the Statesmen, his "day" job was rebuilding pianos for Rich's Department Store. At one time he also sold pianos and organs.

Full-time ministry had been his dream, but it seemed an unrealistic one. At the time, the only people who worked full-time in gospel music were either singers or music editors for the leading publishers. He had already forsaken singing, and he didn't seem cut out for the office tedium of editing. For one who wanted to write gospel music for a living, he had no role models.

Mosie had tried publishing his songs through existing publishers, but those attempts always ended unhappily. That drove him to begin his own Mosie Lister Publications in 1953. But in the beginning, his writing and publishing responsibilities were in addition to a "regular" job.

His frustration built until one day in 1955, when his wife, Wylene, asked him, "If you are called to write gospel music, why don't you just quit your other jobs and do it?" Mosie answered that he had a wife and two daughters to support.

Wylene assured him that the Lord would provide, then prayed with him. That same day Mosie resigned from the Cable Piano Company, and he has done nothing but write gospel music ever since.

During that same year, 1955, he wrote "How Long Has It Been?" "Then I Met the Master," "Where No One Stands Alone," and "Goodby, World, Goodby." He has always viewed those songs as God's encouragement to his faith.

But the traumatic times continued. Wylene was seriously ill, and the doctors urged them to move back to Tampa to be closer to relatives. Should Wylene not survive, their help would be needed with the twin girls. To make matters worse, Mosie's mother died during the move.

There were financial pressures as well. Mosie Lister Publications had been started on very little money, and very little was coming in. But that began to change suddenly. George Beverly Shea recorded "How Long Has It Been?"—Mosie's first recording by a major, nationally known artist. Before long, tens of thousands of printed copies were being sold all over the country. It was the first of his songs to sell sheet music up into six figures. But many others followed, such as "Then I Met the Master," "Where No One Stands Alone," "The King and I," "Goodby, World, Goodby," "He Knows Just What I Need," "His Hand in Mine," "I'm Feeling Fine," "I Won't Turn Back," "The Gentle Stranger," "If You Believe," and "I'm Bound for the Kingdom."

Wylene not only encouraged Mosie to go into full-time songwriting, she worked alongside him, keeping the books, wrapping packages, and helping with the many other day-to-day tasks of the publishing business. She is still a key part of Mosie's life and ministry: "She has stood by me and encouraged me and prayed for me. She has hurt when I hurt, she has rejoiced when I rejoiced—she has been with me through good times and bad."

Merger with Lillenas Publishing Co.

With God's help, Mosie Lister Publications was successful. But one day in 1969, Mosie got a call from Bob Stringfield, then director of Lillenas Publishing Company.

"Mosie, when are you going to get tired of doing your own printing and selling and let us do it for you?"

Mosie told Bob that his call was strangely timed. He had indeed had a particularly difficult day. More than that, the daily demands of running a publishing business were proving an excessive drain on Mosie's songwriting abilities.

Bob said, "Come to Kansas City, and let's talk." And after six months of mutual prayer and soul-searching, Mosie Lister Publications merged with Lillenas Publishing Company. The move not only freed Mosie to concentrate more on his writing, but it brought him to a whole new challenge: writing music for the church, especially church choirs.

Numerous publications combined Mosie's songwriting and choral arranging abilities. There were choral collections like "Gospel Country," "Hallelujah Celebration," "Grace and Glory," "Ever New," "Hallelujah Fountain," "Living Waters," and "Revival in the Land." Volunteer choirs were also given seasonal cantatas: "Reason to Rejoice," "Everlasting Lord," "Love, Light, and Life," "Rock of Faith," "My Faith Still Holds," and others.

Mosie has not "retired," nor does he have any plans to slow down. Several major choral projects pour from his pen every year, and the fresh ideas are still flowing.

Part of the cast of Mosie Lister's "Man of Destiny," a musical drama on the earthly ministry of Jesus. In costume for a 1982 Nashville premier are, standing, L. to R.: Danny Gaither, Sandi Patti, Floyd Parker, Cynthia Clawson, and Rusty Goodman. Kneeling: Mosie Lister with son-in-law Jimmie Vann, who assisted in the creation of the drama.

Tributes

Numerous tributes to Mosie Lister have come in through the years. Hovie Lister, cooriginator of the Statesmen Quartet, says of Mosie:

"He is a great Christian gentleman. Mosie always displayed good clean morals. Not that he was around trying to be a holy joe or somebody that you couldn't live with or get along with, but you just knew where Mosie was. He was just a wonderful person and a wonderful Christian."

Steve W. Mauldin, who has long worked with Mosie as an orchestrator and engineer, and who coproduced the *Good Ol' Gospel* recording, writes: "It was an honor for me to lend my efforts to this tribute album. I know of no one who has given more classic literature to gospel music or who has had more influence on its development than the man who the producers, singers, and musicians of this recording honor, Mosie Lister."

On April 27, 1975, the Riverside Baptist Church of Tampa, Florida, recognized Mosie's unique work in the Body of Christ by ordaining him to the Gospel Ministry. One year later, the Gospel Music Association added their voice by inducting him into their Hall of Fame.

The most moving tributes come from those thousands upon thousands whose lives have been forever changed by the warm, simple gospel truth found in Mosie Lister's songs. And those transformed lives will continue to multiply as long as gospel music is sung.

The Lister family in 1992. Seated, L. to R.: John with father Jimmie Vann (grandson and son-in-law); David Williams (son-in-law); Jason Vann (grandson); Barbara Williams (daughter); Wylene (wife); Mosie. Standing: Marla Williams (granddaughter); Brenda Vann (daughter); Laura Sue Williams (granddaughter).

Mosie Lister Shares
THE STORIES BEHIND HIS SONGS

How Long Has It Been?
(written 1955)

I sweat blood over most of the songs I write. I work very hard at making them what I think they ought to be. But "How Long Has It Been?" was one of those rare exceptions that almost seemed to write itself. It came to me quickly and easily. The writing took a little more than 10 minutes, and this is how it happened.

I grew up in a very religious Christian home where the children always said their prayers at night—"Now I lay me down to sleep," etc. And we learned to express ourselves to God in other ways. It occurred to me one day that there were no doubt many adults who grew up with that kind of experience as children. I wondered if I couldn't say something in a song that would ask if they still remembered praying when they were little; if they still remembered that God heard those prayers; if they remembered telling God, "I love You." I wondered about asking, "How long has it been since you prayed like that?"

All of a sudden I realized that this was what I needed to say. I just started writing as fast as I could. I had the words and music in a little over 10 minutes and before long had the whole song done. Later I felt disappointed with one chord and changed it, but that was the only change I made. Yet this song has been instrumental in God's kingdom, and I'm very thankful.

[Editor's note: Albert E. Brumley once said that "How Long Has It Been?" was the greatest gospel song. Someone asked him, "What about your 'I'll Fly Away'?" To that Mr. Brumley replied, "It's not in the same class with 'How Long Has It Been?'"]

'Til the Storm Passes By
(published 1958)

This song was written because a friend of mine in New York called one day and asked me to write a song for a particular artist. I had enough information about the artist to know that she had had some hard times and bad tribulations early in her life, and I felt I could identify with that.

So, I started writing to comfort people who had been through hard times and bad tribulations. I tried to say that there is hope beyond this life, and there is even hope in this life. I wrote the first verse and chorus, then wrote the third verse. But I thought that something else needed to be said, so I added the second verse.

My mother's thoughts and expressions concerning Christian living made a lasting impression on me. I recall many of the things she said, and they have served me well. She loved to talk about the Bible and about how people needed to serve the Lord. Many times she said that Satan will tell you things you don't need to hear. He will try to discourage you and tell you that there is no need to keep on trying. If he can convince you, he has won. And you don't need to let him win. That's where the second verse came from:

> *Many times Satan whispered,*
> *"There is no need to try,*
> *For there's no end of sorrow,*
> *There's no hope by and by."*
> *But I know Thou art with me,*
> *And tomorrow I'll rise*
> *Where the storms never darken the skies.*

The artist for whom this song was written never sang it. I believe she passed away before she ever saw it. But it has been sung in so many places for so many occasions. I guess every time I hear it, I ask myself, "Did I really write that?" It just seems like something that I didn't write, but I did—with God's help and guidance.

Where No One Stands Alone
(written 1955)

I had been to a gospel concert in Macon, Georgia, and was driving back home to Atlanta, about 90 miles north. It was around midnight, just me, the car, and the road. I was listening to the tires on the pavement, not really thinking about anything that I can recall.

All of a sudden I found myself singing the chorus to what became "Where No One Stands Alone." I started at the beginning of the chorus and sang it all the way to the end. When I reached the end, I realized that I was singing something brand-new, yet something that somehow I already knew. So I went back and sang it again and again. It was almost as if I was singing along with someone else. I had the feeling that there was a choir and orchestra, and I was just a part, maybe a small part, of something that was happening . . . something new and original. I really didn't know just what it was, and that was all I had for about a year—just that chorus.

Then I started struggling to find something to complete what I knew was a song. One evening I was reading Psalm 51 about David's spiritual and mental agony over his sin with Bathsheba and having her husband killed. He was trying to say something to God that would show that he was sorry for his sins. I could tell that David felt so alone, so completely away from God—just totally alone.

That idea all of a sudden gripped me, and I yelled to my wife, "I'll be back in a few minutes." I went out the front door and walked around the block. By the time I came back, I had both verses in mind and wrote those down. In the verses I tried to get inside David's turmoil and say something about how alone he felt, about how we can feel alone if we are far away from God.

At the Crossing
(published 1961)

I wrote this song because I wanted to go beyond "Where No One Stands Alone" and continue its thought into the hope of an afterlife. That idea seemed important—that we want to be one with God when we leave this life. The two songs were intentionally written in the same musical style as well.

Happy Rhythm
(published 1953)

Some songs are just so much fun. I don't know if "fun" is a good way to describe a gospel song, but "Happy Rhythm" is just that. It is fun to sing, and people have always seemed to enjoy hearing it.

It was built around Jim "Chief" Wetherington's voice, of the Statesmen Quartet. "Chief" had a marvelous bass voice, as everyone knows, and I knew him so well. I knew every inflection that he was going to use in a song. I knew how he could anticipate certain notes and sort of lean

into them. It was always a challenge to create new rhythms and sounds for him.

I remembered some things from my childhood about rhythms that certain people were using. I grew up listening to a lot of spirituals that were sung in those days by what we called "Black choirs." Their rhythm was so infectious and so captivating (and the word "fun" comes in here again) that I decided to use kind of a boogie pattern.

The phrase "rockin' and rollin'" had not yet found its way into so-called popular music. I don't know where that phrase came from, but I remembered it from my childhood—though not from music. I just decided I could say, "there's a happy rhythm that keeps rockin' and rollin'." It worked. It was poetic, it bounced, and it was easy to say. I started with the chorus, and it almost wrote itself. Then I went back and wrote two verses and made them easy. I wanted to say, "Brother, let me tell you how I feel, tell you about a feeling that's real"; then, in the chorus, say, "There's a happy feeling that keeps rockin' and rollin'."

Upon completing the song, I immediately showed it to the Statesmen, and they learned it at their next practice session. That same week they had a concert in a high school in Griffin, Georgia, not too far from Atlanta, and they asked me to go along with them. At that concert they introduced "Happy Rhythm." I had never seen a standing ovation before—I didn't know what they were. People just hadn't gotten into doing it. But Hovie Lister introduced "Happy Rhythm" with some of his typical exciting words, and they sang it. People stood up and applauded and yelled and stood in their seats. The guys sang it at least once more, and I was amazed at how the song affected that crowd. They just absolutely loved it.

Then I Met the Master
(published 1956)

This song has been such a comfort to so many people, and at the same time kind of a challenge. At first I didn't realize it was going to be that. I wrote it because I wanted to describe what happened to Jesus' disciples. They were living one kind of life before they met Him. Then after they met Him and knew Him, they lived a completely different kind of life. That's what I wanted to say.

Once I got into writing the song, I realized it was getting emotional (and a lot of my songs are emotional; that's the way I am. I try to say what is true and right, and I try to say it in an original way, using some phrases that haven't been used a lot). So I began by comparing my former state with a blind man that cannot see, and with a baby who is more or less helpless; then saying that all things were different after I met Him, because after I met Him, I realized that I completely belonged to Him.

There is a sad yet beautiful story that I heard just a few years ago. A young teenager in Bradenton, Florida, passed from this life to the next singing this song. When I heard that story, I absolutely wept. I don't know which phrase she sang last, but I was glad that song was a comfort to her. I felt she might have been clinging to the last phrase, "Now I belong to Him" . . . because she did.

This song has also been instrumental in causing some people to commit their lives to the Lord, and causing some to answer the call to preach. It's just been used in many marvelous ways. God has taken it and done far more than I ever thought could happen.

His Hand in Mine
(written 1953)

I was fooling around on the piano, just playing chords and little melodies. I wasn't trying to write anything, just having a little fun in my own mind with my limited keyboard ability. After a bit I found myself playing what became the melody to "His Hand in Mine." I played it all the way through, then played it again. It stuck in my mind, and for a year, every time I sat down to play the piano, I would automatically start playing that little melody. It was easy to play, and it fit my hand. I liked it, but I didn't have any words. I wondered if I could write words for it, but for a time, I couldn't even come up with an idea.

One day while returning from a town about 70 miles southwest of Atlanta, I started thinking about the fact that I just couldn't write words to that melody. Then I remembered an old pastor friend of mine saying that there are times when you need to talk to God like a friend, like an older brother. You've got to use common, everyday, plain old English and just say exactly what you feel. I thought, that's what I'll do.

I stopped the car by the side of the road and said, "Lord, I hope You are listening, and I believe You are. I have this melody, and I've been trying to write words to it and just don't have any words. I have no idea what to say. I don't have a title; I don't have a single word. If it is Your will for this song to be written, I ask You to write it for me, because I simply cannot do it in my own strength. I give up. If You want it written, just write it. Tell me the words, and I'll write them down."

I started the car again and drove home. By the time I got there, I had all the words in my mind, title and all. I went into the house and took my guitar and played it. I sang it to my wife, and she loved it. But there were two or three little spots that bothered me, so I didn't show it to anyone for several weeks. I eventually rewrote the beginning of the chorus but otherwise didn't change anything.

I showed it to some friends who were professional singers and asked them to try it and let me know what they thought. My impression was that it didn't excite anyone. After about a year, a couple of singing groups finally recorded it, but nothing special happened to it. Then, a few years later, a new pop singer by the name of Elvis Presley recorded it and used it as the title to his first gospel album. I didn't even know he knew the song. Since then, it has been established as a standard in Christian music.

I'm Feeling Fine
(published 1952)

I used to listen to a particular group on the radio in Atlanta. They had a first tenor who liked to sing real slow songs and get at the top of his range and just croon, with voices backing him up. I thought: I would love to write a song in that style.

The song was built around the title idea, "I'm feeling fine because I've got heaven on my mind." I don't know where it came from. But I wrote the tune imagining what that particular high tenor could sing if he were crooning a real slow song.

A few days passed, and no one saw it until I got a call from Urias LeFevre of the LeFevre Trio. He asked if I had any new songs, and I said I had one. I took it over to their home, and they started working on it. I didn't know they had recorded it until a month or two later. One day I heard it on the radio, and it was fast—it was really fast. At first I was shocked and thought they had completely ruined my song. But they sounded like they were enjoying it, and it moved along quite well. They started doing it on personal appearances, and other people began picking it up and singing it.

The Blackwood Brothers went to New York to

sing on the "Arthur Godfrey Show," and they sang it on national television the week they were there. It just spread from one thing to another. It's that good old word "fun" again—it was fun to sing, and people enjoy it.

Thanks, Eva Mae LeFevre. If you hadn't taken my slow song and sung it fast, I don't think anyone else would have ever listened to it.

His Grace Is Sufficient for Me
(published 1965)

This song was literally a gift from God. In the mid-1960s, I realized I had gone for an incredibly long time without writing anything that meant anything. It had been over a year, and that was rare for me. Though I sometimes worked on songs for several months, I never thought they were difficult to write, and I had never been through a dry spell like that before. I began feeling somewhat despondent about it. Then I felt I needed to search my mind and my heart, which I began to do.

We were living in Tampa then, and one morning I was driving down to town to get my mail. On the way I started thinking about how long it had been since I had written anything, and I just sincerely and honestly prayed to God. I told Him that I felt that I might be at a place in my life where He was pointing me to do something other than write music, as much as I loved it and felt it was given to me from Him. I told Him that I was despondent over not writing anything and didn't understand why. I said, "Right now I just give You whatever ability I have. If You want me to go in another direction and leave writing, I'll do that and will be happy about it. I just need to know what Your will is. If You'll show me Your will, I'll do it."

After returning from town, I did what I was

doing a lot back in those days. I took my guitar and sat down and just started strumming and humming to myself. I found myself singing, "Many times I'm tried and tested as I travel day by day . . ." I was on the second verse before it dawned on me what I was doing. It occurred to me that this was a new song, and I hadn't written one in over a year.

I thought of the verse of scripture where Paul says, "My grace is sufficient for you" (2 Corinthians 12:9). That became the chorus. Since then, I've never doubted that I'm doing exactly what He wants me to do. I felt that this song came along at a time when I needed its message myself.

Goodby, World, Goodby
(published 1955)

I just wanted to write a happy song about a Christian soul departing this world for the next one. The Statesmen looked at it but didn't especially like it. They seemed to think it was too plain or ordinary. So a few days later I wrote a "jazzy" arrangement of it that I felt expressed what the song was. They ran through it and fell in love with it. It worked. It stuck and became a standard.

In 1992, through the efforts of Bill Gaither, a new Statesmen Quartet was born, and they recorded "Goodby, World, Goodby" as the first song on their first album. It sounded so much like the original version, it was downright eerie. When I first heard them do it, I thought, "My goodness, that's the old Statesmen all over again!" But of course, it wasn't. Hovie was playing the piano and Jake was singing melody, with the other voices working with them. That made it work. They had pretty much recaptured that old sound, thanks to the genius of Bill Gaither.

35

All-time Favorite Songs

by Mosie Lister

1 Goodby, World, Goodby

Words and Music by
Mosie Lister

1. I've told all my trou-bles good-by, Good-by to each tear and each sigh. This world where I roam can-not be my home; I'm bound for a land in the sky. I walk and I talk with my Lord; I feast ev-'ry-day on His word. Heav-en is near, and I can't stay here. Good-by, world, good-by.

2. I won't have the blues an-y-more When I step a-cross to that shore. And I'll nev-er pine, for I'll leave be-hind My heart-aches and tears ev-er-more. A day, may-be two, then good-by; To-mor-row I'll rise up and fly. Heav-en is near, and I can't stay here. Good-by, world, good-by. Now don't you

Then I Met the Master

2

Words and Music by
Mosie Lister

I've Been Changed

3

Words and Music by
Mosie Lister

While Ages Roll

Words and Music by
Mosie Lister

5

His Hand In Mine

Words and Music by
Mosie Lister

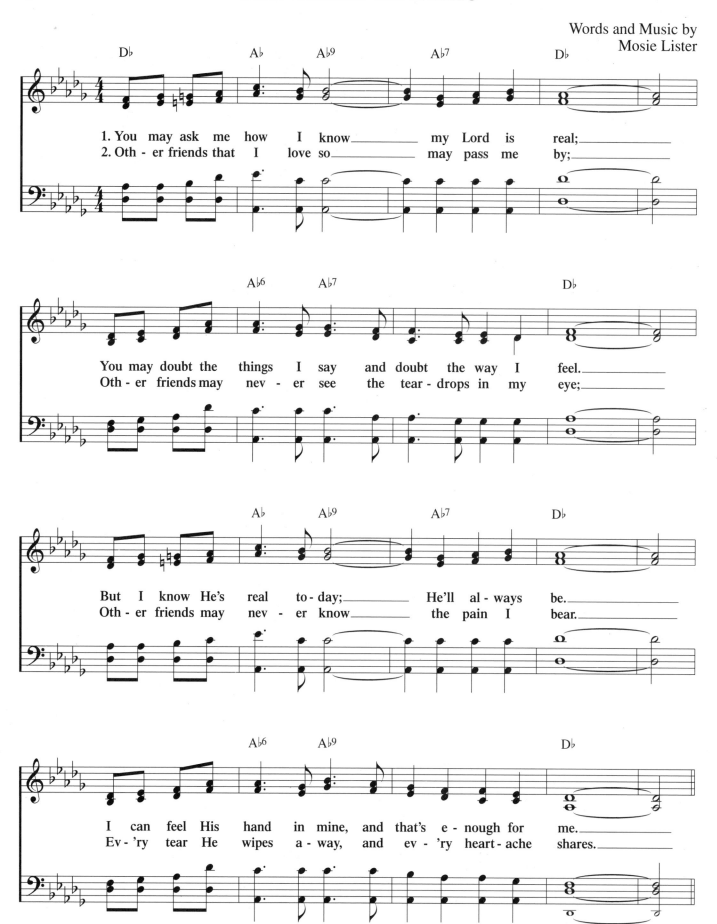

1. You may ask me how I know_____ my Lord is real;_____
2. Oth - er friends that I love so_____ may pass me by;_____

You may doubt the things I say and doubt the way I feel._____
Oth - er friends may nev - er see the tear - drops in my eye;_____

But I know He's real to - day;_____ He'll al - ways be._____
Oth - er friends may nev - er know_____ the pain I bear._____

I can feel His hand in mine, and that's e - nough for me._____
Ev - 'ry tear He wipes a - way, and ev - 'ry heart - ache shares._____

I'm Feeling Fine

Words and Music by
Mosie Lister

1. Well, I woke up this morn-ing feel-ing fine; I woke up with heav-en on my mind. I woke up with joy in my soul, 'Cause I knew my Lord had con-trol. Well, I knew I was walk-ing in the light, 'Cause I'd been on my knees in the night, And I'd prayed 'til the Lord gave a sign, And

2. I've been walk-ing with Je-sus all the time; We're walk-ing and talk-ing as we climb. We're trav-'ling a road to the sky, Where I know I'll live when I die. He's been tell-ing me all a-bout that land, And He tells me that ev-'ry-thing is grand, And He says that a home will be mine, And

CHORUS

Well, I'm feel-ing, feel-ing might-y

now I'm feel-ing might-y fine.
now I'm feel-ing might-y fine.

Feel-ing might-y fine,

7   'Til the Storm Passes By

Words and Music by
Mosie Lister

1. In the dark of the mid-night have I oft hid my face,
2. Man-y times Sa-tan whis-pered, "There is no need to try,
3. When the long night has end-ed and the storms come no more,

While the storm howls a-bove me, and there's no hid-ing place.
For there's no end of sor-row, there's no hope by and by."
Let me stand in Thy pres-ence on that bright, peace-ful shore.

'Mid the crash of the thun-der, pre-cious Lord, hear my cry;
But I know Thou art with me, and to-mor-row I'll rise
In that land where the tem-pest nev-er comes, Lord, may I

Keep me safe 'til the storm pass-es by.
Where the storms nev-er dark-en the skies.
Dwell with Thee when the storm pass-es by.

CHORUS

'Til the storm pass - es o - ver, 'Til the thun - der sounds_ no

more, 'Til the clouds roll for - ev - er from the sky,_____

Hold me fast; let me stand in the hol - low of Thy

hand. Keep me safe 'til the storm pass - es by._____

8

Happy Rhythm

Words and Music by
Mosie Lister

1. Broth-er, let me tell you, tell you how I feel, Tell you 'bout a feel-ing,
2. There is mu-sic ring-ing deep with-in my soul, I can feel it bub-ble,

feel-ing that is real; Broth-er, let me tell you how the glo-ry rolls,
I can feel it roll; Then I get the feel-ing that I want to shout,

Tell you how it bub-bles in my hap-py soul; Hap-pi-ness is free, it's nev-er
Makes me feel so good I've got to move a-bout; Broth-er, there could nev-er be a

bought or sold, Let me tell you how I feel, let me tell you.
sin-gle doubt, I can feel it, I can feel hap-py rhy-thm.

CHORUS

Ta ta ta! Ta ta ta! Ta ta ta! Ta! Ta! Ta ta ta! Ta ta ta!

There's a hap-py rhy-thm keeps a-rock-in' and a-roll - in', I can feel it mov-in' when I

Ta! Ta ta ta! Ta ta ta! Ta ta ta! Ta ta ta! Ta! Ta!

sing this song;_____ What a thrill to feel it mov-in' on and nev-er stop-pin',

Ta ta ta! Ta ta ta! Ta ta ta! Ta! Ta! Roll-in' and a-rock-in' and a-

Deep with-in my heart it keeps a-roll-in' and a-rock - in';

rock-in' and a-roll-in', It's the hap - py rhy-thm in__ my soul,____ in my soul.____

9

How Long Has It Been?

Words and Music by
Mosie Lister

1. How long has it been since you talked with the Lord, And told Him your heart's hid-den se-crets?_____ How long since you prayed? How long since you stayed, On your knees 'til the light shone through?_____ How long has it been since your mind felt at ease? How long since your heart knew no bur-den?_____ Can you call Him your friend? How

2. How long has it been since you knelt by your bed And prayed to the Lord up in heav-en?_____ How long since you knew that He'd an-swer you, And would keep you the long night through?_____ How long has it been since you woke with the dawn, And felt that the day's worth the liv-ing?_____

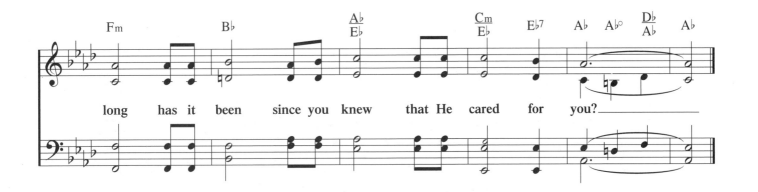

long has it been since you knew that He cared for you?_____

Hard Trials Will Soon Be Over

Words and Music by
Mosie Lister

1. My trials will soon be o-ver, I'll cross the chill-y Jor-dan, And
2. The road is of-ten rug-ged, The load is of-ten heav-y, But

1. My trials so hard will soon be o-ver, I'll cross right o'er the chill-y Jor-dan, And
2. The road I walk is of-ten rug-ged, The load I bear is of-ten heav-y, But

there in Heav-en's Cit-y I'll sit me down,_____ sit me down;___ I'll
soon my feet shall stand_up-on high - er ground,_____ high - er ground;___ Each

there some-where in Heav-en's Cit-y I'll sit me down,_____ sit me down;___ I'll
soon I know my feet shall stand_up-on high - er ground,_____ high - er ground;___ Each

wear a crown of glo - ry, I'll shout the hap-py sto-ry, My
tear I'll leave be-hind_ me, I'll shout good - by to trou-ble, My

wear that day a crown of glo-ry, I'll shout and tell the hap-py sto-ry,
tear and care I'll leave be-hind_ me, I'll shout and say good-by to trou-ble,

OPT. FINAL CHORUS

11 At the Crossing

Words and Music by
Mosie Lister

1. There's a riv-er some-where that's called Jor-dan,_____ And they say that it's
2. Tho' the riv-er is dark_____ and storm-y,_____ It will pass like a

deep and it's wide;_____ And they say that the King and the beg-gar_____ On that
dream in the night;_____ And my soul will a-wake in the morn-ing_____ In_____

shore will stand side_____ by side._____ CHORUS At the cross-ing_____ of the Jor-dan,_____
re-gions of end-less de-light._____

_____ Why should I be a-fraid? There'll be Some-one there who loves me to

guide me_____ 'cross the riv-er_____ To end-less joys_____ a-bove._____

Where No One Stands Alone 12

Words and Music by
Mosie Lister

1. Once I stood in the night with my head bowed low, In the
2. Like a king I may live in a pal-ace so tall, With great

dark-ness as black as could be; And my heart felt a-lone and I
rich-es to call my own; But I don't know a thing in this

cried, "O Lord, don't hide Your face from me." CHORUS
whole wide world that's worse than be-ing a-lone. "Hold my hand all the

way, Ev-'ry hour, ev-'ry day, From here to the great un-known.

Take my hand; Let me stand Where no one stands a-lone."

13 The King and I

Words and Music by
Mosie Lister

1. The King and I walk down life's road to - geth - er
2. The King and I not long a - go were stran - gers.

___ Where man - y peo - ple ___ go pass - ing by;
___ I walked a - lone, ___ not know - ing why,

___ The great - est One and I, a low - ly beg - gar,
___ Un - til He came and put His arms a - round me;

___ Walk hand in hand, ___ the King and I.
___ Now we're not stran - gers, ___ the King and I.

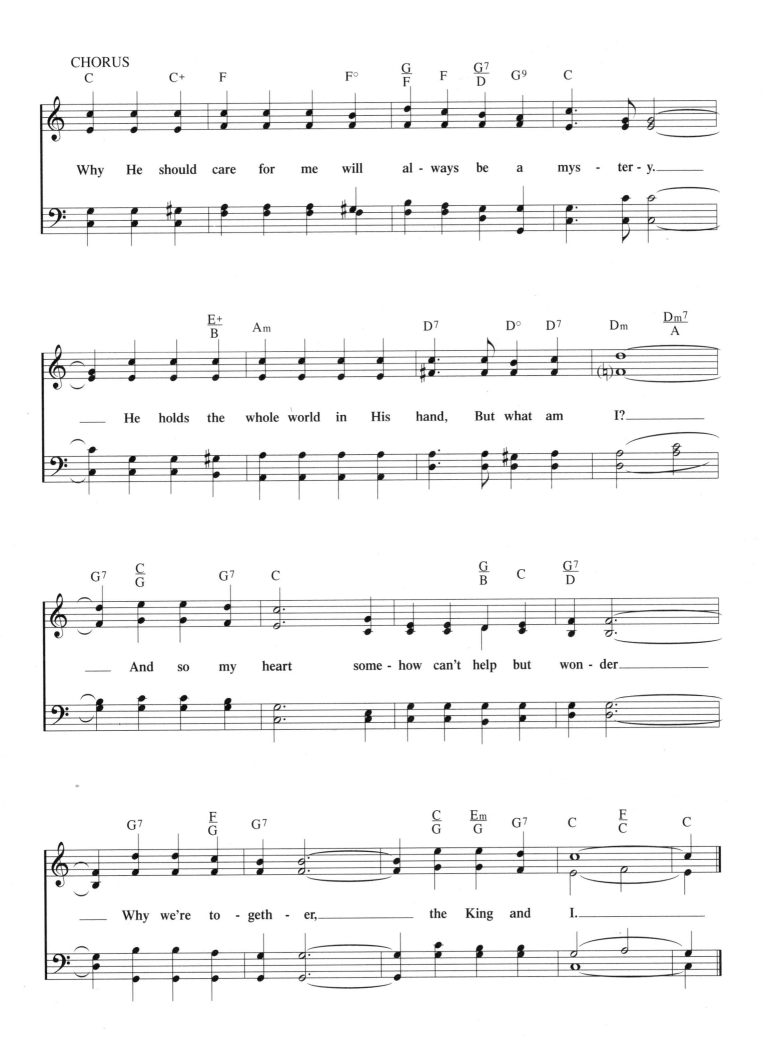

14 Blow Your Trumpet, Gabriel

Words and Music by
Mosie Lister

1. This old world's a-rock-ing, Reel-ing and a-rock-ing, How it keeps on stand-ing I don't know;_____ Lift up your voice and shout, "Ga-briel! Take up your horn and blow."

2. Ga-briel's stand-ing read-y, Stand-ing with his trum-pet, How soon he will sound_ it I don't know;_____ You bet-ter run and hide, sin-ners, For soon he's gon-na blow.

CHORUS
"Blow_____ your trum-pet, blow;_____ Come, Ga-briel, blow your horn._____ Let_____ the whole world know_____ it's time for judg-ment morn." Run,_____ they're gon-na

15 Come and See the Man

Words and Music by
Mosie Lister

16 Down on My Knees

Words and Music by
Mosie Lister

17 His Grace Is Sufficient for Me

Words and Music by
Mosie Lister

1. Man-y times I'm tried and test-ed as I tra-vel day by day; Oft I meet with pain and sor-row, and there's trou-ble in the way. But I have the sweet as-sur-ance that my soul the Lord will lead, And in Him there is strength for ev-'ry need.

2. When the tempt-er brings con-fu-sion and I don't know what to do, On my knees I turn to Je-sus, for I know He'll see me through. Then de-spair is changed to vic-t'ry, ev-'ry doubt just melts a-way, And in Him there is hope for ev-'ry day.

18 Good Old Gospel Singing

Words and Music by
Mosie Lister

1. I recall a slender steeple, A church house filled with people, And voices lifted up in happy song, In music so inviting, So warm and so exciting, I had to enter in and sing along. Then as I joined right with 'em, What harmony and rhythm! My heart was lifted up to heav'n above. I felt like shouting,

2. —With voices lifted high We'd sing "Sweet By and By," And "Rock of Ages, cleft for even me;" "I love to tell the story Of Jesus and His glory;" "Alas and did my Savior bleed for me?" "Lord, send the old-time power;" "I need Thee ev'ry hour;" And "Nothing but the Blood can make me whole;" "O happy, happy

Real - ly swell the cho-rus; Let that hap-py sound pro - long. Ev - 'ry-
bod-y sing it; Make it ring un-til the whole world sings a - long.

19 It's Alright Now

Words and Music by
Mosie Lister

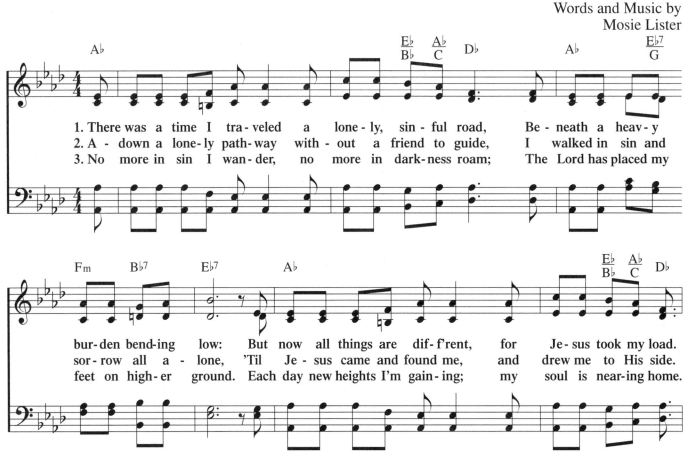

1. There was a time I tra - veled a lone - ly, sin - ful road, Be - neath a heav - y
2. A - down a lone - ly path-way with - out a friend to guide, I walked in sin and
3. No more in sin I wan - der, no more in dark - ness roam; The Lord has placed my

bur - den bend-ing low: But now all things are dif-f'rent, for Je - sus took my load.
sor - row all a - lone, 'Til Je - sus came and found me, and drew me to His side.
feet on high - er ground. Each day new heights I'm gain-ing; my soul is near-ing home.

20 I Won't Turn Back

Words and Music by
Mosie Lister

1. One day when I was walk-ing thro' a drear-y, sin-ful land,
2. The load that once I car-ried is gone for-ev-er-more;
3. He'll help me cross the val-leys and climb the moun-tains tall.

I met a gen-tle stran-ger, who took me by the hand;
My steps that once were fee-ble are bound for heav-en's shore.
He'll nev-er let me stum-ble; He'll nev-er let me fall.

And then I heard Him whis-per, I heard Him call my name,
I'll keep on climb-ing up-ward till I re-ceive my crown,
I mean to stay be-side Him till I reach heav'n-ly ground.

And I knew with all my heart and soul I'd nev-er-more be the same.
But un-til that hap-py, hap-py day I just won't turn a-round.
I won't look to the left, look to the right, And nev-er-more turn a-round.

21   I'll Leave It All Behind

Words and Music by
Mosie Lister

1. I've been blue the whole day through;___ I've been griev-ing all the day.
2. On this road a heav-y load___ I must bear while trudg-ing on;___

Think-ing of the land I love___ Makes be want to fly a-way.___
When I fly a-bove the sky___ I will nev-er walk a-lone.___

CHORUS

Down here I walk___ in sin and sor-row;___ A heav-y load___ of care is mine.___

But when I leave___ this world of sor-row,___ I'll leave it all be-hind.___

For ev-'ry tear___ and ev-'ry heart-ache, For ev-'ry mile___ that I must roam,___

22 I'm Bound for the Kingdom

Words and Music by
Mosie Lister

1. You may ask me where I'm head-ed; you may ask me
2. Well, I'm go-ing to a coun-try where they say we'll

where I'm bound. Well, I'm go-ing to a coun-try
nev-er die. 'Twill be end-less joy and glo-ry

'cross the sea; And I know I'll have a
there for me; Yes, I know I'll live for -

man-sion, and I know I'll have a crown.
ev-er in that cit-y in the sky. Well, I'm

bound for the King-dom of the free.

23 I'm Climbing Up the Mountain

Words and Music by
Mosie Lister

24

Oh, What a Friend

Words and Music by
Mosie Lister

Nothing Can Compare

25

Words and Music by
Mosie Lister

26 When They Call My Name

Words and Music by
Mosie Lister

melody in alto

1. Some morn-ing soon I'm gon-na take to the air,____ I'm gon-na
2. It won't be long 'til I shall hear the trump sound,____ It won't be

Some morn-ing soon
It won't be long

leave this world of sor-row and care;____ I'll hear the
long 'til I shall leave this low ground;____ My heart with

I'm gon-na leave
It won't be long

wel-come bells all ring-ing, Home-ward I'll be wing-ing When they call my name.____
glad-ness o-ver-flow-ing, Home-ward I'll be go-ing When they call my name.____

CHORUS

Some of these morn-ings they'll be call-ing my name,____
Some morn-ing they'll be call-ing my name,____ They'll call me

27 The Way of the Cross Led Me Home

Words and Music by
Mosie Lister

28 The Touch of His Hand

Words and Music by
Mosie Lister

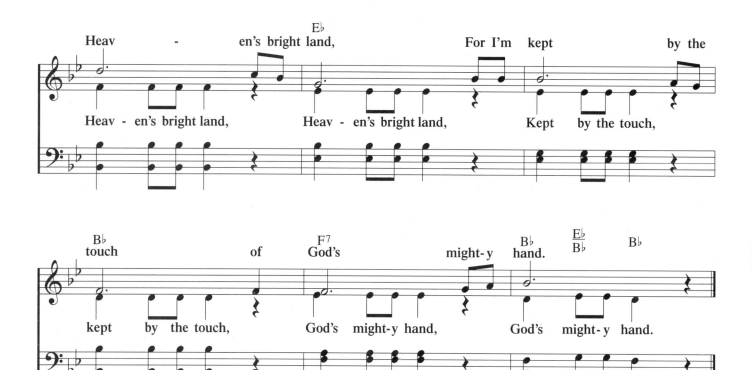

Heav - en's bright land, For I'm kept by the

Heav - en's bright land, Heav - en's bright land, Kept by the touch,

touch of God's might-y hand. kept by the touch, God's might-y hand, God's might-y hand.

29   When I Inherit My Mansion

Words and Music by
Mosie Lister

1. My Lord has told of a man-sion That I'll in - her - it some -
2. This fal - t'ring tongue can't de - scribe it; No words can tell of its

day, A home of won - der and beau - ty, In heav - en,
worth; To show its grace and its beau - ty, There is no

The Gentle Stranger

Words and Music by
Mosie Lister

1. Once as I walked a-lone A-down a lone-ly road,
2. Then as He whis-pered low Such things I'd longed to know,

And had no one to bear my sor-row or my blame,
My heart re-joiced to know the won-der of His grace.

A gen-tle Stran-ger came, And took me by the hand,
I've learned to love Him so, And this I sure-ly know,

And some-how ev-'ry care de-part-ed when He came.
He'll be no Stran-ger when I see Him face to face.

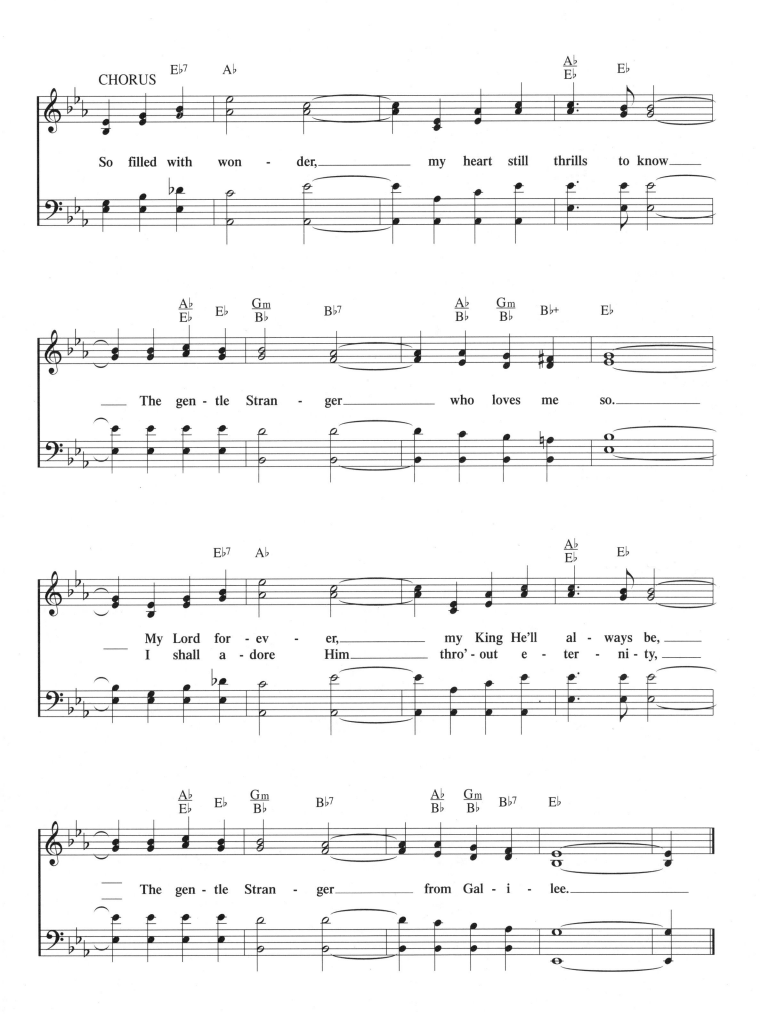

31 Restore My Soul

Words and Music by
Mosie Lister

1. Lord, You know that I've been fool-ish, I've been blind;
2. Stripped of all that once I clung to, Lord, I come;

I've let my doubts and my con-fu-sions cloud my mind.
Tho' in Your eyes I know I'm noth-ing, yet I come.

I have walked in my own wis-dom; I've been wrong.
With your hand that once was nail-scarred just for me,

Take my hand and lead me back where I be-long.
Touch me now and make me all that I should be.

CHORUS

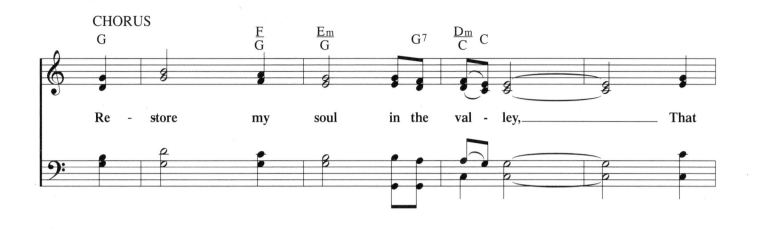

Re - store my soul in the val - ley,_____ That

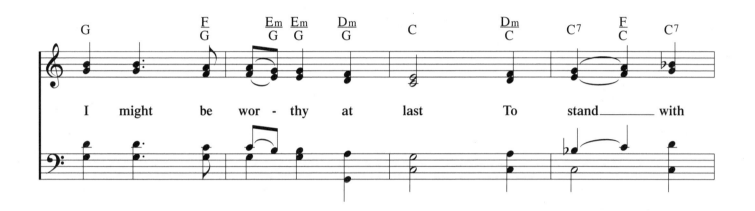

I might be wor - thy at last To stand_____ with

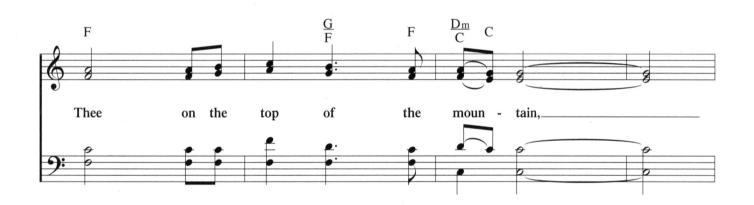

Thee on the top of the moun - tain,_____

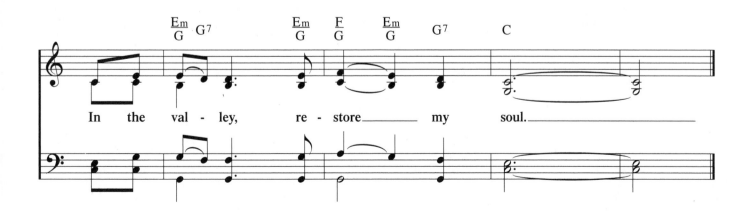

In the val - ley, re - store_____ my soul._____

32   In the Arms of Sweet Deliverance

Words and Music by
Mosie Lister

If You Believe

Words and Music by
Mosie Lister

1. I read a-bout (I read a-bout) how Paul and Si-las were in jail,
2. When Dan-iel sat (When Dan-iel sat) with-in the hun-gry li-on's den,
3. When Da-vid stood (When Da-vid stood) be-fore the gi-ant with his sling,

And no one there, (And no one there) no-bo-dy there could go their bail.
No-bod-y tho' (No-bod-y tho') that there was an-y hope for him.
Go-li-ath laughed (Go-li-ath laughed) at such a pu-ny lit-tle thing.

But when they prayed (But when they prayed) they found that God was on their side;
But all night long (But all night long) the li-ons nev-er took a bite;
But Da-vid knew (But Da-vid knew) his faith in God would stand the test.

That jail-house door (That jail-house door) swung o-pen wide.____
God took a-way (God took a-way) their ap-pe-tite.____
He flung the rock; (He flung the rock) God did the rest.____

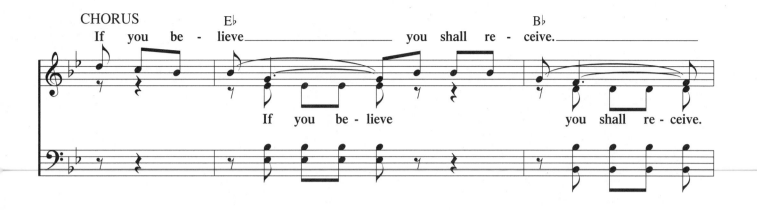

CHORUS

If you be - lieve_____ you shall re - ceive._____

If you be - lieve you shall re - ceive.

There's not a trou-ble or care the good Lord can't re - lieve; Oh,

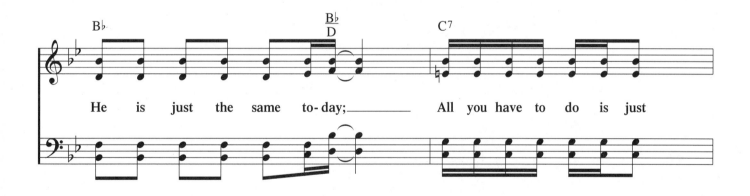

He is just the same to-day;_____ All you have to do is just

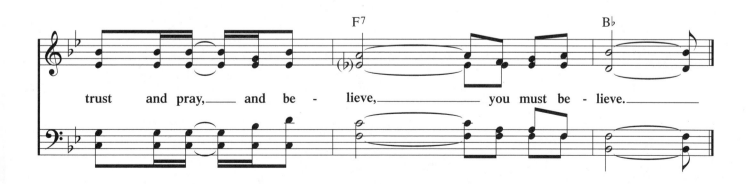

trust and pray,_____ and be - lieve,_____ you must be - lieve._____

34 He Knows Just What I Need

Words and Music by
Mosie Lister

Led by the Master's Hand

Words and Music by
Mosie Lister